Alcimar Emanuel Farias Rodrigues

School indiscipline and the relationship between teachers and students

AF144447

Alcimar Emanuel Farias Rodrigues

School indiscipline and the relationship between teachers and students

School indiscipline

ScienciaScripts

Imprint

Any brand names and product names mentioned in this book are subject to trademark, brand or patent protection and are trademarks or registered trademarks of their respective holders. The use of brand names, product names, common names, trade names, product descriptions etc. even without a particular marking in this work is in no way to be construed to mean that such names may be regarded as unrestricted in respect of trademark and brand protection legislation and could thus be used by anyone.

Cover image: www.ingimage.com

This book is a translation from the original published under ISBN 978-620-2-04922-1.

Publisher:
Sciencia Scripts
is a trademark of
Dodo Books Indian Ocean Ltd. and OmniScriptum S.R.L publishing group

120 High Road, East Finchley, London, N2 9ED, United Kingdom
Str. Armeneasca 28/1, office 1, Chisinau MD-2012, Republic of Moldova, Europe
Printed at: see last page
ISBN: 978-620-7-24409-6

SUMMARY

DEDICATORY

I dedicate this work to all my family and friends as an incentive to always want to be in search of new knowledge, paraphrasing the great educator Paulo Freire, if education is not everything, but without it, the life of the citizen is worse. To my siblings and everyone who has been by my side, sharing in the construction of my knowledge.

To my God who gave me life and the constant courage, perseverance and faith to travel in this crazy, thirsty world. To HIM be all honor and glory. Life goes on all the time. I build my world by traveling in other worlds that sometimes stay and sometimes leave.

I dedicate it to my mother, Maria de Fàtima Farias Rodrigues, who has always given me her unconditional support.

I dedicate it to my father, Alcimar Batista Rodrigues, who is my inspiration and role model.

I dedicate it to my sisters, whom I can always count on regardless of the circumstances.

I dedicate it to my great friend, Keveny Ribeiro Lemos, who accompanied me during this stage. This is truly a brother I have gained from life.

Finally, to everyone who, directly or indirectly, contributed to this milestone.

The educator or group coordinator is like a conductor conducting an orchestra. By coordinating in tune with each different instrument, he or she conducts everyone's music. The conductor knows the content of the scores for each instrument and what each one can offer. The harmony of each with the other, the harmony of each with the conductor, the harmony of the conductor with each and everyone is what makes the pedagogical piece possible. This is the art of governing differences, socializing individual knowledge in the construction of generalizable knowledge and for the construction of the democratic process.

Freire, in: Aguiar, 1999, p. 115

SUMMARY

School indiscipline is certainly one of the biggest problems facing Brazilian schools today, a problem that puts our country in a very low position when compared to other countries.

This work is a research project, the purpose of which is to observe and collect bibliographic data on the relationship between teachers and students and the influences exerted on disciplinary issues in secondary schools.

Crime, media influence and lost values are all common causes of school indiscipline. A student's act of indiscipline often comes from those who are doing badly at school, perceive themselves as excluded beings in the learning process, feel humiliated, and therefore decide not to agree with what is on offer.

What we hear most often in schools is that students: "don't want anything to do with anything, don't care about their own future, their parents aren't committed to their children's education and development, moral values have been lost", in short, a variety of complaints that most of the time place the student as the protagonist of this indiscipline. But to what extent can the student be held responsible for indiscipline in the school environment?

Key words: school indiscipline, teacher-student relationship.

1. INTRODUCTION

School indiscipline is certainly one of the biggest problems facing Brazilian schools today, a problem that puts our country in a very low position when compared to other countries.

There are several factors that we can point to and cite as possible causes of school indiscipline, such as stressed teachers, unbelieving and discredited students, failed teaching, physical and psychological violence, a large number of failures, students dropping out and the neglect of families in accompanying their children in their education process, leaving education to the schools. "... Very often, the family doesn't educate, doesn't give basic references and transfers this task to the school..." (Vasconcellos, 2013).

This work is a research project, the purpose of which is to observe and collect bibliographic data on the relationship between teachers and students and the influences exerted on disciplinary issues in secondary schools.

The disrespectful practices and bad behavior of undisciplined students are influenced from the family environment to the school institution, and when solutions, support and partnerships are not sought, indiscipline can be the trigger for violence. Disobedience, lack of respect and disorder are common problems reported by teachers at different levels of education. School indiscipline has been experienced intensely in the daily lives of educators, and is the subject of   discussion among education   professionals. Often our

educators are very apprehensive about the problem, creating   a situation of anguish in the school environment.   Many say that discipline and

have given way to bewilderment and indifference among students and educators.

Crime, media influence and lost values are all common causes of school indiscipline. A student's act of indiscipline often comes from those who are doing badly at school, perceive themselves as excluded beings in the learning process, feel humiliated, and therefore decide not to agree with what is on offer.

Indiscipline in the school environment has been seen as one of the biggest problems hindering teaching and learning in schools today. The main factors that generate indiscipline range from the influence of society to students' family life, which creates circumstances that lead students to deviant behavior. The school's position as a mediator of knowledge in the face of indiscipline is to realize that it is not necessary to change the people who work in the school, but rather the attitudes taken towards these students. What we hear most often in schools is that students: "don't want anything to do with

4

anything, don't care about their own future, their parents aren't committed to their children's education and development, moral values have been lost", in short, a variety of complaints that most of the time place the student as the protagonist of this indiscipline. But to what extent can the student be held responsible for indiscipline in the school environment?

According to Aquino (1996), the teacher-student relationship is very important, to the point of establishing personal positions in relation to methodology, assessment and content. If the relationship between the two is positive, the likelihood of greater learning increases. The strength of the teacher-student relationship is significant and ends up producing varied results in individuals.

2. OBJECTIVES:

2.1 General objective

Bibliographical analysis of changes in the teacher-student relationship and their influence on discipline in secondary schools.

2.2 Specific objectives

> To see if the teacher's approach in the classroom influences the student's behavior.

> Specify the best attitude for teachers to adopt in the classroom.

> Investigate the reasons why students act aggressively and become unruly.

3. THEORETICAL FRAMEWORK

To approach this topic, let's first look at the concept of discipline in order to understand the term indiscipline.

According to Mendes (1995), the concept of discipline stems from a particular conception of children, adults and adult-child relationships. In short, it stems from the concept of man, society and knowledge that is assumed.

Indiscipline is not defined by itself, it arises as the negation of something, whether that something is an accepted social norm or standard or an arbitrarily imposed rule.

But does being disciplined only mean being obedient, quiet and submissive? This concept needs to be reviewed and reconsidered, because participation, restlessness, the reconstruction of concepts and behaviors are essential attitudes for meaningful learning. The concept of indiscipline is of great magnitude and complexity, as Garcia (1999) and De La Taille (1996) point out. When analyzing the concept of indiscipline, we must take these aspects into account. Another aspect we need to consider is overcoming the notion of indiscipline as something restricted to student behavior, since the subject requires, according to Oliveira (2004), deep reflection on the nature of the relationships and interactions that constitute it.

The notion of indiscipline will be considered taking into account three specific situations of occurrence. Firstly, it is embedded in the conduct of students in various educational activities, both inside and outside school. On the other hand, it appears in the dimension of the socialization processes and relationships experienced by students, in relation to their peers and education professionals, in the school context with its pedagogical activities, heritage, environment, etc. And finally, indiscipline appears in the context of students' cognitive development. Thus, indiscipline can be defined as the incongruence between the criteria and expectations assumed by the school (which reflect the thinking of the school community) in terms of behaviour, attitudes, socialization, relationships and cognitive development and what the students demonstrate in terms of their social context.

Finally, it is possible to understand indiscipline as something that originates in the teacher-student relationship. And that it always implies the contravention of principles, regulations, contracts and orders, clearly disagreeing with the objectives of the group or institution and causing situations of disturbance to social relations within it (AMADO, 2001). I would also point out that, according to Amado (2001), the concrete manifestation of indiscipline is the failure to comply with the rules that govern, guide and establish the conditions of the tasks and also the disrespect for the norms and values that underpin healthy coexistence between peers and the relationship with the teacher as a person and authority.

If we consider the history of humanity, we will realize that the search for social control is something ancient. According to Professor Marilena Chaui (CHAUi 2000), the problem of indiscipline and the means to prevent and control it has been around since ancient times. But we also see in many historical moments the abuse of power in the pursuit of social control or discipline. Fortunately, this idea of power and punishment has lasted for centuries; until recently, physical punishment of the body was common in schools, such as the spanking.

According to Aquino (2000), everyday school life at the beginning of the century mirrored barracks, where the teacher was a hierarchical superior with the function of morally modelling the students, similar to a militarization, teacher and students had defined roles.

According to Aquino (1996), the democratization of education took place in the 1970s, and with the demilitarization of social relations, a new generation was formed, the students are new historical subjects, but we still keep the image of that submissive and obedient student as a pedagogical model.

3.1 The factors behind indiscipline in the school environment

Research into this problem has attributed the causes to various factors, such as: a reflection of poverty and violence; problems in their social environment; parents who are uninterested in their children; the age of the student interfering; or the teacher being blamed.

It is essential to understand that individuals develop according to their social internalization, their culture. Therefore, indiscipline and discipline are learned. As such, the family exerts a great influence on the behaviour of indiscipline or discipline in the student, since it is the first form of socialization of the individual, where culture and values are passed on. Following the line of thought of Vygotsky apud Aquino (1996), the individual develops according to the environment, in which the family and social environment structure the subject's behavior.

The school environment is seen as an ideal place for training and preparation in all dimensions of the human being: psychological, social, political and so on. When not well prepared for these dimensions, the student, who is endowed with a set of values and expectations that vary throughout history, brings disorderly conduct into the classroom, such as messiness, turmoil, disrespect for the teacher, lack of limits, bad behavior, in other words, failure to comply with the rules established by the school. All of this behavior is called indiscipline, which is increasingly manifesting itself in schools, making it an obstacle to the work of the educator and the performance of the students, and in turn exposing education to danger. Indiscipline is indicative of a structural deficiency in the student's inner psyche, determined by institutional transformations in the family and leading to school relationships (AQUINO, 1996, p. 48).

The classroom is the privileged place where relationships are woven between teachers and students, and between the students themselves. It is there that the group is formed, the collective, which is not always respected by the teacher, since the latter doesn't always feel part of the group, but someone from outside with the power of command, and the sole holder of knowledge. Guimarâes (1996, p.78), when talking about the classroom, says that: "The classroom is the place where a network of relationships is woven. To the extent that the teacher is unable to perceive this web, he or she concentrates the conflicts either on him or herself or on a few pupils, and does not move them to the collective. As there is no reversibility of   positions, a rigid division is formed between those who know and those who don't.

who imposes and the one who obeys and rebels. In this way, everyone is driven by an order, by an obligation that is imposed and not incorporated."

The teacher tries to maintain order in the classroom by centering responsibility for discipline on his or her own, and in many cases, overbearing, position. Due to the diversity of elements that make up the classroom, it is impossible to maintain this position. This rigid form of organization, where the teacher is in charge and the students obey, the latter being considered not to be the holders of knowledge, makes it easier for acts of indiscipline to erupt. Therefore, as the students are not considered co-participants in the teaching process, which implies the division of responsibilities in building a peaceful space in the classroom, the authoritarianism of the teacher prevails, who seeks to maintain discipline without reflecting on his authoritarian practice.

The teacher's role is important not as the central figure, but as the coordinator of the educational process, since, using democratic authority, he or she creates interesting, stimulating and challenging pedagogical spaces together with the students, so that meaningful school knowledge can be built.

It is necessary that the necessary form of communication is established between peers for meaningful learning to really take place. Vasconcellos (2003, p. 58) says that: The teacher plays the role of model, guide, reference (whether to be followed or challenged) in this

9

process; but students can also learn to deal with knowledge from their peers. One thing is "ready-made", systematized knowledge, but quite another is this knowledge in movement, influenced by the questions of existence, being assembled and disassembled (conceptual engineering). You learn to think, or, if you like, you learn to learn.

The teaching profession requires constant negotiation, both when it comes to defining objectives and teaching and assessment strategies, and when it comes to discipline, which, if imposed authoritatively, will never be accepted by the students.

Students spontaneously and unplannedly seek to live, which makes the classroom marked by difference and precariousness. They are continuous bearers of novelties, coming from the family in the lack of limits for their children and the consequences of this for school and learning.

There is a conflicting relationship between the teacher and the student: the student does not accept the teacher or their subject and the teacher or their subject fails to motivate, there is no standard strategy to apply when faced with a student's attitude.

As society becomes more democratic and the authoritarian instruments it has placed at the service of the school are eliminated, the relationship of obedience becomes clearer, because relationships are no longer based on respect and subjects no longer feel obliged to comply with rules (AQUINO, 1996 p.36).

School indiscipline ranges from not wanting to lend a classmate an eraser to the extreme of talking when not asked to, including, of course, the well-known resistance to sitting properly at one's desk (LAJONQUIÉRE, 1996).

This path can begin when a student is wronged, and rebels against the authorities who victimize them, in a non-physical way, in swearing, and can reach physical form, finds it difficult to make friends and socialize their ideas with other classmates, these manifestations can often be made by the undisciplined student as a way of showing their existence to the world, where rebellion is a form of expression.

So let's beware of condemning indiscipline without having examined the rationale behind the rules imposed and the behavior expected, and without having considered the age of the students: you can't demand the same behavior and understanding from 8-year-olds as from 13 or 14-year-olds (LA TAILLE, 1996).

Students, like teachers, also want to be treated with respect. There are teachers who underestimate their students, rush through content thinking it won't be missed, make misdiagnoses and all this can be a reason for students to express their anguish with unruly

10

acts.

Is a nice teacher, the friend of the class, able or able to maintain respect and organization in the classroom? Do nice teachers generate unruly students? This goody-goody teacher attitude is known to most teachers at the start of their careers. What are the attitudes of a nice teacher that call into question the process to be carried out in the classroom? These questions become pertinent, because when you realize that nice teachers can result in difficult pupils, you may have the mistaken idea that you need to take on the posture of a tough, evil teacher, "with a face like a few friends", that teacher who strikes terror and frightens his pupils.

In some circumstances, it can be seen that the problem lies not in being that good-natured teacher, the one who tries to give a relaxed and fun lesson, but in the lack of definition of rules and behaviors that are desirable for the lessons to run smoothly. No matter how much you reflect on the students' attitudes during lessons, the task of reversing the students' perception of the lack of pre-established rules can be difficult.

A teacher's attitude is necessary:

> Clearly define disciplinary rules.

> Establish, in consensus with the students, the desirable limits of behavior and always enforce them immediately and consistently.

> To demand, firmly but always with good humor, the harmonious cooperation of everyone in complying with the rules of conduct agreed with the class.

> Calmly analyze the reasons why students may be disinterested or undisciplined and discuss this with them.

> Take care of its presentation, dignifying the importance and even the sense of the pedagogical act.

> Conclude the lesson in a friendly and humorous manner.

Tiba mentions that: "The environment also interferes with discipline" (TIBA, 2006, page 128).

School indiscipline is also due to the place that schools occupy in society today. They are often ill-equipped to deal with the complexity of today's problems and end up producing their own indiscipline, for example: how spaces, time and networks of relationships are

11

shared, which, when the teacher is unable to perceive this web, can lead to conflicts and divisions of opinion in the group. "When a child falls and doesn't want to be picked up, maternal indiscipline occurs when the mother picks the child up because she did what she wanted to do, without researching what the child wanted". (TIBA, 2006, p. 41).

If the child finds fertile ground at home, it will become a rebellious plant at school, and then expand into society (Tiba, 2006, p.159).

Aquino says: "In both ways, indiscipline presents itself as a symptom of discontinuous and conflicting relationships between the school space and other social institutions."

The family is the basis for everyone to live well in society, it is the security to face any variable, but if for some reason the family breaks down, or lives in conflicts, it will be like the reason for indiscipline to exist in a child, causing directly in the school space and in society.

Aquino points out, "Limits: children today would not have limits, parents would not impose them, schools would not teach them, society would not demand them, television would sabotage them, etc.". (AQUINO, 1996, p. 9).

Tiba, writing about adolescents and indiscipline, says:

> "They need financial, legal and emotional support from their parents and they detest adults - gods, insecure, bossy, authoritarian, repetitive, fickle, cold or arrogant - much more than at other ages." So the origins of indiscipline are not always their own fault. They can be reactions and a lack of tolerance for what they don't accept (TIBA, 2006, p. 148).

Adolescence is one of the most necessary phases in which parents need to be attentive to their children, and children think that they won't need their parents at all. This is a phase in which they can't tolerate those authoritarian, rigid parents in their children's lives. This type of indiscipline isn't caused by the family, but by some undisciplined reactions to recognizing and respecting their parents' opinions because they are from a different world. "In short, it seems that there are not a few people for whom indiscipline would be a kind of great and ultimate evil, and the quality of the child's psychological capacities, the cause of the causes". (LAJONQUIÉRE, 1996, p. 26).

Family breakdown directly interferes with the student's behavioral and cognitive problems, which are then transported to other social environments, including school (AMADO & FREIRE, 2009). In fact, several international and Portuguese studies have shown that children with more unruly behavior came from families whose parents were more permissive or extremely authoritarian (VEIGA 2001; AMADO & FREIRE, 2009).

12

Especially in the lives of children and adolescents, parents or other significant adults (vertical relationships) and peers (horizontal relationships) are the main references, and there is an interdependence between these two realities: family and school (SCHAFFER, 2005).

This issue brings with it another problem: the "expanded" responsibility of the teacher, who today has to carry out tasks that are not part of his profession, and is sometimes asked to take care of duties traditionally assigned to parents. In this sense, Boarini points out:

> Understanding that the teacher doesn't make the school an extension of the home is another point that deserves revision. They are different roles. The teacher is prepared and specialized over a period of time to share the production and systematization of knowledge with the student. This is what we call professionalization, which must be carried out in line with public education policies. To this day, it has not been said that, in order to exercise maternal and paternal functions, those interested must pass special courses for this purpose. Each parent raises their children in their own way. Even if teachers, especially in the early grades, have to deal with unforeseen circumstances outside their training, this does not necessarily make them a substitute for paternal/maternal or parental functions. They are different roles, although they should be moving in the same direction (BOARINI, 2013, p. 125).

One problem that is evident in most schools is that even with all these new roles for the institution and its members, there are still teachers who follow only the traditional line of teaching.

> (...) there is still a didactic approach which considers the teacher to be the sole holder of knowledge in the classroom. The student must remain quiet and attentive for hours on end. The teacher becomes accustomed to working with the "limits of cannot", instead of privileging the "limits of possibility", not taking into account that the aim of pedagogical work is to "suppress the figure of the student as a student, that is, pedagogical work is carried out in order to make the figure of the student disappear" (CHAUÎ, 2013, p.128). (emphasis added).

Today, we live in a society that no longer needs a static, stationary subject, settled in a certain place, attached to certain social and affective relationships, passive? Instead, we need a flexible, creative, multiple and agile individual, who extends their affective, cognitive and executive possibilities as far as possible (JUSTO, 2010).

> It is education that is prestigious, taking on ever greater roles and responsibilities, becoming the great social institution; however, [...] it cannot

cope with the demands of contemporaneity, nor does it have the necessary instruments to do so. It embraces the subjectivities of this time and has an organizational structure from a very different time (JUSTO, 2010, p. 42).

According to Vasconcelos (2004), the causes of indiscipline are linked to five groups: society, family, school, teacher and student. But, in fact, where is the center of this problem? The student? The teacher? The school? The family? In society? Discipline, according to the author, is a collective construction of pedagogical practice that requires effort, commitment and dedication from everyone involved.

> School discipline or indiscipline is a human prerogative, a complex and uncertain phenomenon. [...] Unruly behavior can be an indication of dissatisfaction within the school institution. The promotion or control of indiscipline in students is not written about in pedagogical or any other literature, nor do we receive formulas for maintaining discipline or avoiding indiscipline with our diploma. Discipline is a necessary exercise in any situation, social or otherwise. In the case of the school environment, discipline is a daily exercise that takes place in the classroom. It must be built and managed on a daily basis by everyone involved in education. This exercise is not a problem for us educators. It is a commitment and a challenge and it is part of our job (BOARINI, 2013, p.129).

Motivation according to Nerici (apud ECCHELI, 2008, p.75) is described as "the process that develops within the individual and drives him or her to act, mentally or physically, for something. The motivated individual is willing to expend effort in order to achieve their goals".

Eccheli (2008, p.199) points out that:

> Getting students to feel motivated to learn is the first step towards preventing indiscipline, and is a major challenge for teachers and schools. Teachers want students who know how to respect their classmates and who are able to engage in activities that require concentration and effort to learn, but this is not synonymous with students who are passive and silent all the time. The silence so desired in the classroom is not always a guarantee of learning, because students learn when they actively participate in an activity, carrying out a task, listening to different ways of perceiving a subject and having the opportunity to argue their ideas through discussion groups or debates. This active participation by students in school activities is an expression of energy and enthusiasm, the fruit of meaningful learning.

This is an arduous task for the educator, who will have to be able to perceive the students' difficulties and needs, including challenging activities in their planning, as well as constantly reflecting on their practice (EC- CHELI, 2008).

> Faced with this impasse, teaching (and disciplining) people who don't want to be subjected by the school, it's up to the institution and the teacher to consciously try to manage power as a force that emerges in relationships, using different instruments from those created in the early days of disciplinary institutions, as these still retained the possibility of using violence as a resource to reinforce their discourse. (DAMETTO; ESQUINSA- NI, 2009, p.9).

1.2   The importance of dialogue in relationships

Let's start by understanding the meaning of the word interaction:

> Interpersonal process by which individuals in contact temporarily modify their behavior in relation to each other, by continuous reciprocal stimulation. Social interaction is the fundamental behavioral mode in groups (DiCIONÂRIO DE PSICOLOGIA, p. 439).

Freire (1987, p.93) emphasizes dialogue as "the encounter between men, mediated by the world in order to pronounce it". He develops a pedagogy based on the process of critical awareness of reality. The author believes that the essence of a problematized and critical education can be built through commitment between people, and that dialogue is an essential part of this process.

> [Dialogue is an existential requirement. And, if it is the encounter in which the reflection and action of its subjects, addressed to the world to be transformed and humanized, are in solidarity, it cannot be reduced to an act of depositing ideas from one subject to another, nor can it become a simple exchange of ideas to be consumed by the exchangers. (FREIRE, 1989, p. 91).

Thus, the more teachers understand the importance of dialogue for good teaching and learning, the better their relations with students will be, arousing interest, removing the teacher as a mere transmitter of knowledge, motivating students to transform their reality.

According to Estela (2002, p. 19-20), schools have undergone many transformations, but it is still common to find what the author calls traditional magisterialism:

> If the teacher has lost the monopoly of knowledge that underpinned his authority and legitimized his charisma, and if his discourse has changed as a result of the multiple social pressures that prescribe other roles for him, in everyday pedagogical practice, many teachers still tend to preserve the central place in the organization of the pedagogical act that traditional pedagogy attributed to them. Thus, they privilege their role as transmitters of

15

knowledge, monopolize or centralize communication by limiting the possibilities for the student-recipient to become a transmitter, create illusory forms of participation and minimize relational aspects [...] they condition feelings by conditioning the possibility of their externalization; they control human relations in the classroom; they determine the criteria of what is good, true, beautiful, useful, correct.

Freller (2008. p. 71) also observes these expectations of teachers in relation to students, i.e. that they be docile, quiet and submissive. These expectations on the part of some educators do not take into account the plurality of individuals who are present in the classroom, each with their own way of learning and relating, including the educator himself.

On the other hand, according to Jesus (2008, p. 22), students are not as influenced by their teacher as they were in the past, when they were idealized as "Mr. Doctor" or "Mr. Teacher". For the author, what makes teachers successful with their students today is their appreciation of certain personal and relational qualities in their teacher. We therefore argue that teachers should be much more attentive to how their personal characteristics may be interfering in classroom relationships. According to the author (2008, p. 22), while previously the student adapted to the teacher's method, today the teacher "[...] must meet the interests and language of the students [...]." The teacher is a leader who must motivate his students, as he states that one of the main consequences of demotivation in the classroom is school indiscipline.

For Furlani (2004), it is necessary to get to know the student, to know how to listen to them, to observe them, to propose teaching methodologies that are compatible with what the student already has, in order to move them forward in their learning, and this can happen through a dialog between the teacher and the teacher and the students, which can most often arise from the practical actions of the teachers, and the actions of the students in relation to the space they are in.

That's why dialog is an essential tool in teacher-student relationships, which, together with hope, are based on an eternal quest to restore humanity crushed by social, economic and educational injustices, among others.

"The teacher's sensitivity enables him to understand the child's developmental stages, making him experience a world of imagination, dreams, joy, etc." (SIQUEIRA ET al., 2011, p.7).

When the teacher dialogues with the student, they are not just trying to get answers they already know. This encourages critical thinking and makes the student reflect in a new way, consider alternative methods of thinking and acting.

Let's look at what was written by LIBÂNEO (1994, p.250):

> The teacher doesn't just pass on information or ask questions, but also listens to the students. They must pay attention to them and ensure that they learn to express themselves, express their opinions and give answers. Teaching is never one-way. Their answers and opinions show how they are reacting to the teacher's actions, to the difficulties they encounter in assimilating knowledge. They also serve to diagnose the causes of these difficulties.

The teacher can't have the attitude of thinking that his or her word is the law, because when there is a breakdown in communication between teacher and student, the two parties can become distant, which can lead to a clash in the relationship; dialogue is a fundamental element of learning. HAYDT (1995, p.87) tells us about the importance of establishing dialogue.

> Dialogue is fundamental in the teacher-student relationship. The dialogic attitude in the teaching-learning process is one that starts from a problematized question, to trigger the dialogue, in which the teacher transmits what he or she knows, taking advantage of the student's previous knowledge and experiences. Thus, both arrive at a synthesis that elucidates, explains or solves the problem situation that triggered the discussion.

To earn the student's respect, the teacher must be aware of the importance of their work and blend their authority with affection, always seeking dialogue as a way of achieving the desired result. We can reinforce the importance of dialogue using Freire (1996, p.95): stimulating questions, critical reflection on the question itself, what is intended by this or that question (...) the fundamental thing is that teacher and students know that their posture is dialogical, open, curious, inquiring and not apathetic, while they speak or while they listen.

1.3 Affectivity

Affectivity goes beyond being understood as affection, love, affection or a psychological state that allows us to show feelings, a bond between human beings. And these feelings exert a force on all of us that generates positive or negative forces. According to Mello, Rubio (2013), affection is affection, love, oriented towards the inner state, feeling, that is, affection is governed by all manifestations and can thus add or detract from a way of acting.

Almeida (2007 p.17) defines affectivity as "the capacity, the disposition of the human being to be affected by the external and internal world through sensations linked to pleasant or unpleasant tones".

For Mello and Rubio (2013), learning is related to factors that go beyond the act of teaching and applying new and creative methodologies. For these authors, affection is a determining factor in learning and the educator's role is also to make students aware of themselves in society, knowing how to accept themselves and others. "Learning takes place through social interactions and these originate through the bonds we establish with others, so it can be said that all learning is imbued with affectivity" (GOLDANE, 2010, p.13).).

Learning is a combination of emotional, pedagogical, biological and other factors, and school learning is the basis for a student's development (MAIA org, 2011). This social environment of feelings that will intervene in the learning process is details in a school day that will define the influence on learning (MAIA org, 2012).

"The teacher's sensitivity enables him to understand the child's developmental stages, making him experience a world of imagination, dreams, joy, etc." (SIQUEIRA et al., 2011, p.7).

> The student sees in the teacher the chances of a more consistent path in the search for cognitive fulfillment if the teacher represents positive affection, the necessary support, constituting a protective factor in the school environment. It is important to emphasize that affective aspects and a positive teacher-student interaction play a preponderant role in the affinities that develop between teachers and students in "liking the teacher". (GOLDANI, 2010, p. 29). (emphasis added).

It is in the classroom that students must have their needs met so that this can be transformed into the intellectual conditions for learning; it is where dialog, coexistence and relationships take place (SIQUEIRA et al, 2011). Alves (2000) highlights the teacher's joy in teaching, in loving what they do:

> Teaching is an exercise in immortality. Somehow we continue to live in the one whose eyes have learned to see the world through the magic of our words. The teacher thus never dies (ALVES, 2000, p.5 apud MELLO; RUBIO, 2013, p.6).

Mello and Rubio (2013, p.7) state that "small gestures such as smiling, listening, reflecting and respecting are, among many others, necessary for the child's adaptation, safety, knowledge and development". "The teacher must influence in a positive way, highlighting

18

strengths in their character that awaken in the student a   desire to learn, to want to acquire values and virtues, transforming them into a critical citizen" (SIQUEIRA, ET AL, 2011, p.9).

1.4 Psychosocial factors that influence indiscipline:

The family: When we talk about the family, we are not necessarily referring to the traditional concept, with the presence of a father, mother and children.   family model is no longer a reference for our children. The family environment we are referring to is the one in which the child lives with someone who is responsible for him or her, which could be parents, grandparents, uncles, siblings, godparents, among others, because it is these people who the child will look up to as an example and who will influence his or her conduct.

The media: When parents try to encourage children to have an upbringing based on moral and ethical values, the media, television and social media, tend to make this difficult. TV stations, through their unscrupulous programming, whose sole aim is to increase their ratings, encourage rebellion, competition, individualism, sex and violence.

> Violence is transmitted to children through cartoons, to young people through films and to adults through the news, leading to a trivialization of violence and aggression, with indiscipline in the classroom being one of the manifestations of this situation (JESUS, 1999, p. 48).

Many times, teachers come across scenes of violence among students and don't realize that they are just reproducing at school what they have seen on TV or websites, whether in films or cartoons. Cases of teenagers shooting and killing classmates and innocent people after watching movies and compulsive killing stories on TV are not uncommon in the news, both at home and abroad.

Diversity: When we talk about diversity, we are referring to the different cultures we encounter in the school environment. We know that even in public schools on the outskirts of town, which cater for children from the same community, there is no such thing as homogeneity, since all people have feelings,   desires, ambitions, beliefs and values, and are imbued with customs and practices that they   acquire in their family and social environment (ways of acting, language, gestures,   attitudes, hygiene habits) which form their personality   from an early age. Education professionals must be prepared for what is different and know how to deal with these situations, sometimes unconsciously, as accepting the behavior of a   student whose attitudes and customs show proximity to their values, in other words, to what they   think is right.

19

1.5 Pedagogical factors that influence indiscipline:

Imposition or lack of rules: In certain situations, the school rules are not even explained or discussed with the students. When a new school year begins, there is no clarification from the educators about what is expected of the students, nor is there any guidance on the conduct that will ensure that the teaching/learning process runs smoothly, such as respect between those involved in daily school life.

Perhaps this lack of guidance is because not even the teaching team is clear about the principles that should guide student behavior. Often, there is no prior discussion between teachers at the school to reflect and make joint decisions about this. This lack of guidance means that each teacher acts in the way that suits them best, using only their experience and common sense.

The teacher's pedagogical proposal: The absence of a well-developed pedagogical proposal can be another determinant of indiscipline. The content taught and the methodology used often don't match the expectations and reality of the students, in other words, the students can't understand why they should learn certain subjects that make no sense to their daily lives. It is necessary for the teacher to adapt the students to the reality they live in or to their needs.

> Another very common example is mathematics, which is usually taught in a mechanical way, causing most students to find it very difficult to understand and to have an aversion to this subject (CARRAHER, T.; CARRAHER, D; SCHLIEMANN, 1993).

This problem arises from the fact that, unfortunately, some teachers don't know how to justify the need to teach certain content, which ends up with them using vague content that doesn't attract students' attention, with the excuse that it's a compulsory subject on the syllabus or that it will be on the exam.

1.6 Classroom conflicts that generate indiscipline:

As Debarbieux (2002, p. 66) points out, Dubert characterizes school violence as a "climate of indiscipline that is paradoxically more tangible than the acts that generate it" and with which, in turn, school participants live and are affected. Through this discourse, we cannot present a problem without studying its causes or contributors. Given this logic of discussion, as Fernândez (2004) shows, in a process of   discussion and disagreements generated at school between students - students, students and teachers,   not   only those who develop violence, be it physical or verbal, are   involved,   but   also   those (teachers, management and the school board) who contribute in some way to the acts by

20

omitting or failing to punish those involved for any type of violence or indiscipline committed against people within the school. In fact, these conflicts or disagreements between pupils, pupils and teachers and even between parents and teachers, children and parents, are inevitable and in some cases even desirable. It is true that they can be resolved without the need to use verbal aggression or even physical violence, as stated by Coll and others (2004). However, these two types of aggression are present both inside and outside the school environment. In this context, according to Coll et al. (2004), it is important to take into account the phenomenon of gratuitous violence that occurs between two or more people who play different roles: the aggressor and the victim. Generally, this type of violence, according to the author (p.124), reproduces "a form of relationship in which the aggressor behaves as a dominator" and takes pleasure in sacrificing their victims with insults, threats, lies or physical violence. In many cases, there are no other motivations for the aggressor   than the pleasure of "doing".

to undermine, to attract attention". In the school environment, this type of aggressor is classified as "the bully", the one who always wants to demonstrate his dominating role.

In the same way, verbal aggression often arises from attempts to resolve conflicts through dialogue. Despite this, these conflicts become even bigger and more complicated to resolve, depending on the way they are resolved or the loss of emotional balance of the participants, generating a real educational   perversion, in which learning to resort to violence to resolve conflicts becomes for the aggressors the easiest way to resolve them, and ends up complicating the situation even more. This inability to resolve conflicts is the result of a degraded moral, social and psychological upbringing which is reflected in the family, school classes and groups of teachers, according to Coll and others (2004).

As a result of these aggressive and violent behaviors in the classroom, teachers, parents, principals, school coordinators and even some students are concerned about finding alternatives to alleviate the problem. In these cases, it is important to note that some European studies treat the problem of school violence as oscillating points between individual psychological aspects (behavioral problems) and sociological aspects (unemployment, social exclusion, hunger, among others) that end up affecting the emotional and psychic structure of the participants, as Blaya (2002) points out. This author also emphasizes the psychological aspect as one of the most affected due to the production of unwanted behaviors   .

Ana Carita and Graça Fernandes (1995) offer some suggestions for reflection on the process of trying to resolve conflicts and promote discipline in the classroom: punishment, which can lead to the student's behavior becoming that desired by the teacher and which may no longer manifest in the student the previous undesired behavior, but which can also have negative consequences such as increased rebellion, reduced self-esteem and a feeling of rejection; encouragement with rewards for positive behavior, which helps to reduce negative behaviors and attitudes and encourages the development of behaviors necessary for good learning; and the teacher's recognition of his or her positive and negative practices and influences in the classroom, which can help the student control his or her behaviors and conflicts and promote pleasant and desirable behaviors.

These alternatives, however, need to be reflected on in terms of their application and, when applied, their results evaluated. From this point on, we can see the influence and role of the teacher in shaping the student's conduct and its relationship with what can be called theory and practice in an attempt to improve behavior in the training of students. For education, this can be considered a major advance in the field of theories in the search for educational success.

1.7 The educational system and the school:

The educational system imposes a traditional standard of rigid behavior that institutions must follow, which is often out of touch with the particular reality of each school. Even if teachers try to work under these rules, they end up causing tension and demotivating them from any initiative.

Some of the impositions imposed by the school system are common knowledge: overcrowded schools, large classes, broken classroom desks, lack of teaching materials, excessive bureaucratic demands on teachers, unsatisfactory pay, constant changes in educational paradigms, among others. There are also factors relating to the physical structure of the school, such as inadequate and dilapidated buildings, cramped and hot classrooms with little ventilation and lighting, and classrooms that are affected by outside noise. All this will certainly have a negative impact on the students' behavior.

School can hardly be considered a pleasant place and so, for many students, going to school becomes an obligation, since it has no appeal and is imposed by their parents.

We know that education is the responsibility of governments, but, for a long time, they have not invested in it as they should, and this neglect and failure to prioritize education is leading to it being scrapped.

Bringing up a child today is not the same as bringing up a child 40 years ago. Society has changed and families have changed too. Everything around us has much more flexible and loose boundaries. Today, we have widespread indiscipline, authorized by the media, by our culture and by families themselves.

Educators are perhaps one of the few groups on the planet who value, teach and demand from children and young people attitudes based on principles, values and firmness of character.

Are we such "jurassic" and outdated beings that we are one of the few who row and walk against this growing current of corruption, indiscipline, lack of morals, principles and character?

Educators are the ones who point out, teach, correct, charge, but by pointing out we are exposing the negligence and incompetence of families in the correct education of their children, a negligence that has a very high price, and who pays it is society and all those who live or will live in it.

What we see today are children and young people using their headphones, their latest generation cell phones, behaving in a debauched and undisciplined manner, using rude, disrespectful and derogatory language in the classroom, and who often feel authorized to do so by their families, who fail in their duty to educate them.

This behavior is also the fault of the school when it doesn't have mechanisms for effective management of spaces and the creation of standardized disciplinary rules for all teachers, and of the managers who in many cases don't offer the support and backing that the teacher needs in order to apply the appropriate correction.

It is the teacher who ends up becoming the villain of the story, because he is the one who is always "picking on" the students, he is the one who is always complaining about indiscipline in the classroom, he is the one who is demanding compliance with the rules. The negative result of this is that the teacher's discourse becomes lost, suffocated in a tangle of controversial perceptions and values.

Unfortunately, it can be seen that families themselves teach and encourage their children to fight back and not to take "insults home". The children in turn live with parents who shout, physically and verbally attack each other and are not good role models.

Parents need to blame someone for their children's failure, students need to find a "Judas to beat up" and some Managers need a scapegoat to take the blame.

When we enter a classroom, we shouldn't do so naively or unprepared. We're not there just to give lessons or comply with the textbook. We need to be clear about our real role within the larger context of education.

Some ways of dealing with indiscipline in the school environment:

1)   Treating them with indifference and pretending not to care and letting them "ro- lar";

2)   Forcing parents and students, by legal means or with strong measures and threats, to take action in relation to their children's indiscipline;

3)   Create strategies to minimize, circumvent or correct a situation.

We hear a lot about the indiscipline of children and students, and every day parents and teachers are incessantly looking for solutions to this uncomfortable reality. Everyone is clamoring for knowledge on the subject, because we are living in a time when children and young people are mistaken about the values that make up a stable society, with solid values that benefit everyone. Serious and conscious reflection on the current reality is therefore unavoidable.

Imposing limits on children helps them to change their behavior without damaging their self-esteem. According to Maldonado (1986, p. 106), setting limits "essentially consists of 'delimiting terrain'", so that someone else knows where they stand or, in other words, can clearly discern what is permitted and what is forbidden.

Parents or teachers can't be afraid to set limits, make excuses for not doing so or feel insecure about setting limits. These attitudes cause them to lose authority over the rules they impose. Almeida (2008, p. 84) completes this thought by stating that, "when limits are put to the test, the child cannot win. Otherwise they will be sure that they are in charge of the situation".

Indiscipline is one of the most worrying factors in the school system, as it is one of the villains of students' failure to learn. Teachers, in turn, don't know how to deal with issues related to indiscipline, and students who stand out for this type of behavior are treated in a way that generates even more indiscipline or the other extreme, for example, being labeled as hyperactive or rude.

The teacher and, often by extension, the institution itself, don't know how to deal with this issue and put into practice methods such as punishment, which is often applied to children who have not committed the acts to be punished or are unaware of the reasons why they are being punished. Sometimes the school - the professionals who work in the school environment - don't even know why the act of indiscipline occurred.

It's not about finding a "culprit" for indiscipline. It is easier and quicker to solve a problem when someone is blamed; however, both the school institution and the teachers themselves need to stop looking for the culprits and start taking action. In this respect, Vasconcellos (1995, p. 54) points out: "[...] to educate is to break this chain of alienation, to activate the physical and the mind, to develop all logical and affective potential, to make each of the '16 billion neurons' work, true nuclear power plants of creativity". It is clear that "unity is strength"; in other words, family and school need to join forces to solve problems, evaluate methodologies, promote pedagogical meetings to address the issue of indiscipline, so that the curriculum is appropriate to the reality faced by the school environment.

It is the school's responsibility to value educators and offer them better working conditions, promote training meetings, fight for better salaries, establish a number of students per class, provide adequate equipment and restructure methodologies to teach attractive classes in line with the technological modernity that so amazes students. The school must also be flexible when it comes to applying rules, promoting out-of-class activities that aim to help students understand that the rules contribute to the harmonious running of classes and the school context in general.

The mistake of blaming the teacher for indiscipline occurs because the teacher is the person who is in constant contact with the student; most of the time, even more so than the family itself. In view of this, the teacher needs to take on and transform the reality that surrounds him, of which he is both an agent and a patient. Students, in turn, as interlocutors in this process, must participate consciously and interactively, knowing their rights and duties, rules and sanctions, which they themselves can draw up - for example, classroom rules. Vasconcellos (1995, p. 106) says: "The affectivity of a democratic discipline at school ultimately depends on the democratization of society. Educators must commit themselves to the process of transforming reality,

We can highlight five major mistakes made by teachers in the classroom, which end up resulting in indiscipline among their students:

Mistake 1: Disciplining the whole room at once;

Mistake 2: Mouthing off to the student, instead of giving them direction on what to do;

Mistake 3: Threatening, threatening, threatening and not complying;

Mistake 4: Inappropriate use of non-verbal language;

Mistake 5: Boring lesson from start to finish;

25

1.8 Technology can be an ally against indiscipline in the classroom:

Rather than being a source of distraction in the classroom, technology should become an ally for teachers in the teaching and learning process.

Seeing children with tablets, smartphones and laptops is no longer an unusual scene in the classroom. And there is no distinction between public or private schools, primary or secondary. With the spread of technology, these devices have gained a foothold in people's routines and are even in educational institutions.

In order for them not to become points of dispersion during lessons, we need to follow a path of knowledge and collaboration between students, teachers and their families.

Rather than restricting or prohibiting them, teachers need to add these tools to the teaching and learning process. Society is undergoing a change, and connections with the virtual happen in any environment.

In today's scenario, technology is entering schools as a fundamental tool for improving the problems of student disobedience. Some of them are very accessible and can be used to drastically reduce the distance between the school, the students and their guardians.

A good example of this is the school communication apps. Through this platform, even parents with busy routines can control their children's entry and exit times from school, keep track of their children's grades, absences and disciplinary incidents at any time and from anywhere, and can work together with the school to ensure that nothing goes wrong.

Social media such as facebook and whatsapp can be useful tools for bringing families closer to the school, as well as making lessons attractive for students, reducing the doldrums of boring lessons that students hope will end soon.

With parents more present and involved in their children's school life, student performance improves, the school achieves better results and attracts more parents and students interested in the institution. With more enrolments, the school can reinvest in teaching and bring in more technology to encourage students and support teachers, continuing a productive cycle where everyone wins.

1.9 Postmodern children and the challenge of educating them

Children in the 21st century are smarter, more inquisitive, curious about everything and always connected to everything that's going on around them. They are encouraged to play with interactive toys that stimulate quick thinking, their hobbies are with games that use logic and intelligence.

Today you don't see those shy and withdrawn children, but those who know how to talk from an early age, even when they learn to speak, are more coherent, they don't talk as badly as they used to.

However, according to Tiba (2002, p.234), this new generation is incapable "of dealing with frustration, which carries over into social relationships."

If they can't do something that's too difficult, they move on to someone else where they're smarter, and the same goes for relationships. They don't need to get frustrated with someone, they just let go and move on to someone else.

Adolescents are starting their sex lives early, even without affection: if it doesn't work out with this one, it will work out with another. The media and easy access to information mean that these children want to experiment, or rather, prefer to be fashionable, so that they are not excluded from their circle of friends outside and inside school.

A major obstacle that schools face are curious children who watch television and the internet and want to do the same. Many teachers complain about students who make obscene gestures in the classroom. They bring this behavior   from   home   and   are often not observed by their own families. These are not the only worries on the minds of parents and schools, drugs are another intriguing subject. In the same way that sexual activity is initiated by curiosity, drug use also begins in this way.

In this sense, the great challenge of educating them. They have so much information that it's hard to know how and what to teach them first. Parents and schools should therefore keep a close eye on the children, what they watch on TV, where they go on the internet, and who their companies are. This will facilitate teaching and learning and may have a positive impact on their behavior at school.

4. METHODOLOGY

Type of study: This dissertation is a literature review, based on existing data, on school indiscipline and the relationship between teachers and students.

Place of study: The bibliographic research was carried out in online databases such as CAPES, SCIELO and Google Scholar, as well as books available in the digital collection of the Federal University of Amazonas.

Bibliographic strengths: Articles, scientific journals, physical and digital books were used in this research. The key words used were: school indiscipline, teacher-student relationship.

Inclusion and Exclusion Criteria: The research aims to search for textual elements that will be limited to studies carried out mainly in the last ten years on theorists who have published on the subject, seeking a discussion of the evolution of the problem, as well as the methods that could have reduced this indiscipline. Thus, all data that is not directly related to the topic will be excluded from the research.

Data collection: Data collection was carried out mainly in the months of August to December 2016 through works already published in online databases such as CAPES, SCIELO and Google academic, as well as books available in the digital collection of the Federal University of Amazonas.

Data analysis: After data collection, data analysis was carried out, where the main theories and ideas presented on school practice, didactic postures, teacher dominance and, above all, the educator's posture towards the student and their positioning in conflict situations were surveyed and compared.

Table 1: List of the most relevant articles selected for the literature review

Number	Article title	Author	Study site	Year of Publication	Base Consult- da
1	A indisciplineand feeling of shame.	AQUINO	São Paulo	1996	SCIELO
2	Teacher authority: Goal, myth or none of that?	FURLANI	São Paulo	2004	Google Digital
3	Office master:	ARROYO	Petrópolis	2000	SCIELO

	images and self-images			
4	School discipline: prevention and intervention in behavior problems	GOTIZENS	Porto Alegre	2003	SCIELO
5	Education as the practice of freedom	FREIRE	Rio de Janeiro	1989	Database UFAM
6	Stories of school indiscipline	FRELLER	São Paulo	, 2008.	Google Digital
7	Teachers' attitudes towards school indiscipline	OLIVEIRA	Curitiba,	2004.	SCIELO
8	School discipline: prevention and intervention in behavior problems	GOTIZENS	Porto Alegre	2003	SCIELO
9	Strategies to motivate students	JESUS	Porto Alegre	2008	Google Digital

5. PRESENTATION AND ANALYSIS OF RESULTS:

During the preparation of this bibliographical study, the importance of this research topic for the students' school life as well as for the common good of the school as a whole became apparent. In tackling indiscipline in schools, education cannot be seen as the responsibility of schools alone. Everything in society can be and is pedagogical in a positive or negative sense.

In the family, at work, in the media, in political action, in religious acts, in any sector of human activity, we are teaching new generations models and proposals with technical, political and moral content. This is so true in modern society, where children are in contact with the world through television, intense interaction with adults and the internet. Based on this information, a search was made among authors with work carried out in the last ten years, seeking to compare the data and information provided in order to analyze the evolution of this serious problem that schools are experiencing.

In a bibliographical survey, we observed the studies carried out by researcher TATIANE SALVADOR DA CRUZ TAVARES in her article: INDISCIPLINA ESCOLAR E SUA INFLUÊNCIA NO APRENDIZADO (SCHOOL INDISCIPLINE AND ITS INFLUENCE ON LEARNING), carried out in 2012, where the author used data collected through a semi-structured questionnaire applied to teachers, with the aim of finding out their opinions. The following data was obtained:

The parents of some of the students were asked through questionnaires where the first graph asked whether parents participate in their children's school life.

Graph 1: Results of whether parents participate in their children's school life. Research evaluated by Tatiane Salvador da Cruz Tavares, 2012

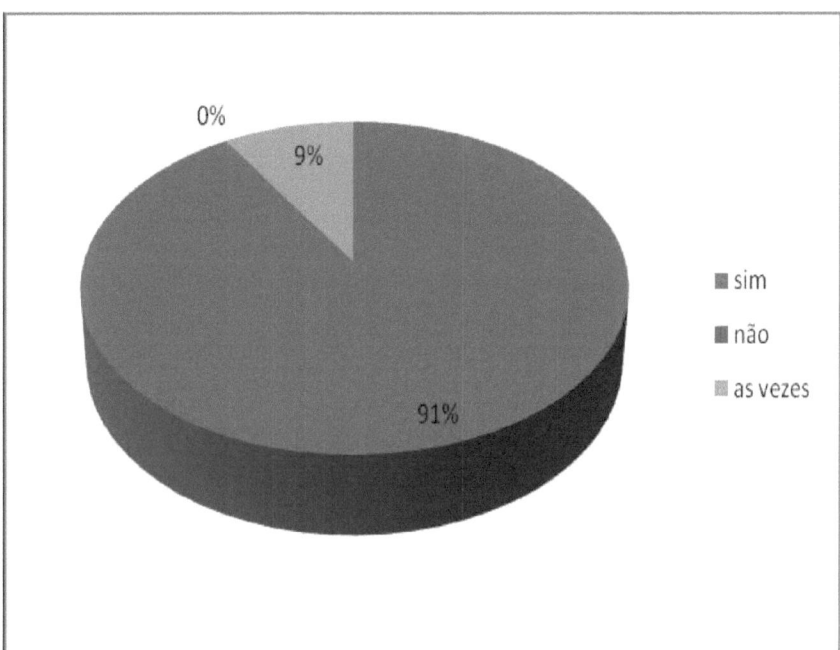

It can be seen that the vast majority of those surveyed, 91% in total, say that they participate in their children's school life, and that only 9% of those surveyed say that they only participate in their children's school life sometimes.

Graph 2: Results of how parents participate in their children's school. Evaluated research by Tatiane Salvador da Cruz Tavares, 2012

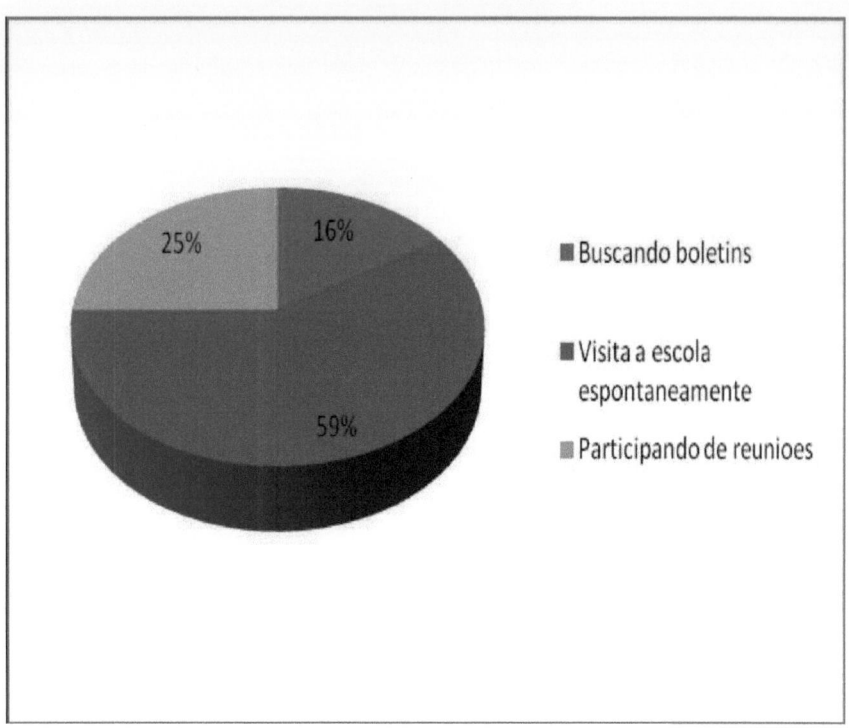

We analyzed that 59% of parents say they go to school spontaneously, 25% only attend meetings and 16% go to their children's school just to pick up their children's report cards.

When it came to the teachers, through surveys and questionnaires the teachers gave the following answers:

Graph 3: Results on whether indiscipline in the classroom hinders the teacher's performance, surveyed by Tatiane Salvador da Cruz Tavares, 2012.

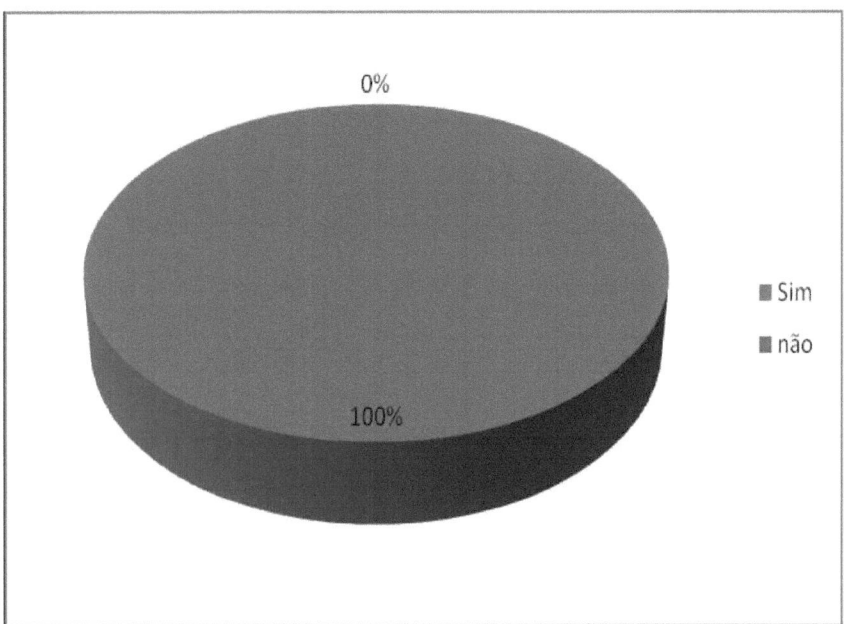

All the teachers said that their students' indiscipline interferes with their own performance in the classroom.

Graph 4: Results of whether students' indiscipline in the classroom is a reflection of their behavior at home. Research evaluated by Tatiane Salvador da Cruz Tavares, 2012.

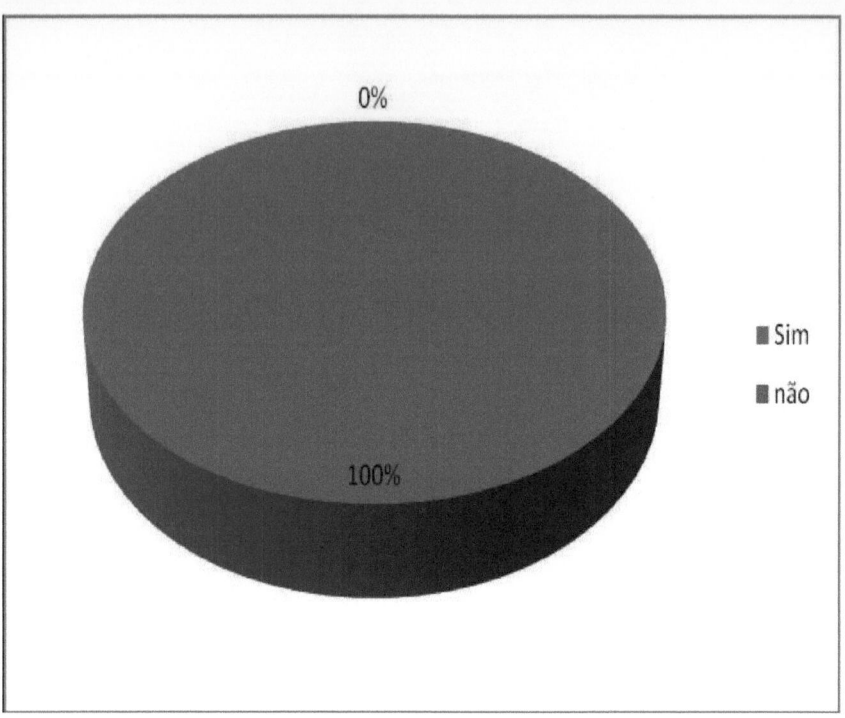

It can be seen that for 100% of the teachers the reflection of the students' behavior comes from the education they receive at home

Graph 5: Causes of school indiscipline. Research by Tatiane Salvador da Cruz Tavares, 2012.

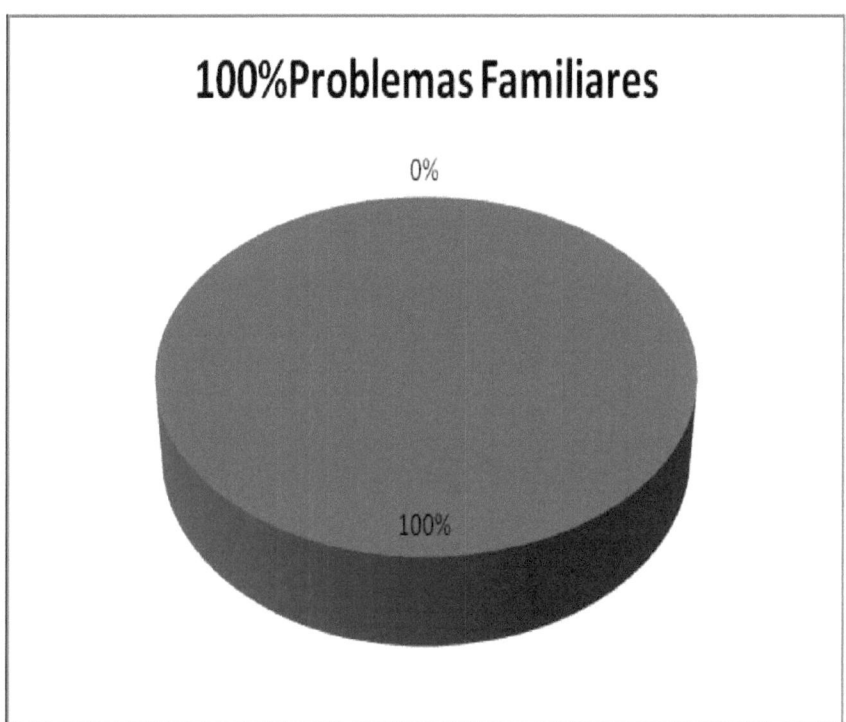

For 100% of the teachers, the causes of indiscipline are: family problems, lack of limits, family breakdown and little family participation in school.

Graph 6: Result if the student's behavior in the classroom takes attention away from his classmates. Research by Tatiane Salvador da Cruz Tavares, 2012.

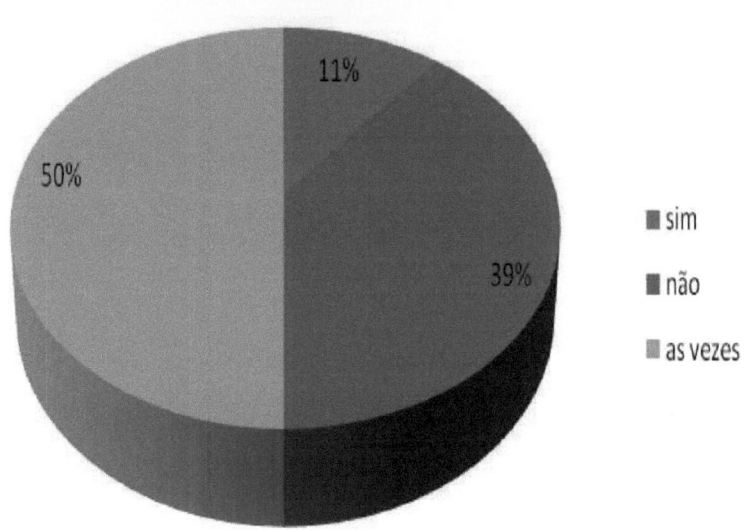

For 50% of the students, their behavior sometimes takes attention away from other classmates, 39% say it doesn't and 11% say it does.

Graph 7: Result if the indiscipline of classmates harms their school performance. Survey by Tatiane Salvador da Cruz Tavares, 2012.

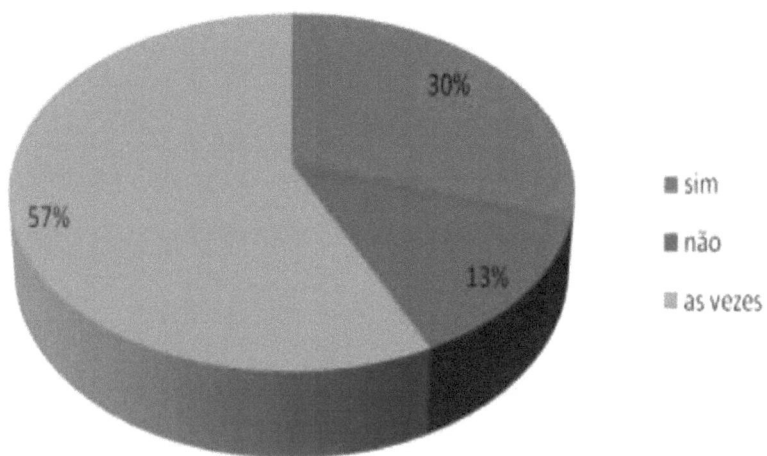

Does the indiscipline of classmates hinder your learning? The answers obtained were: 57% answered that "sometimes" their classmates' indiscipline hinders their learning; 30% answered that "yes" their classmates' indiscipline hinders their learning and only 13% answered that "no" their classmates' indiscipline does not hinder their learning.

Graph 8: Result if students complain about indiscipline in the classroom to their parents. Research by Tatiane Salvador da Cruz Tavares, 2012.

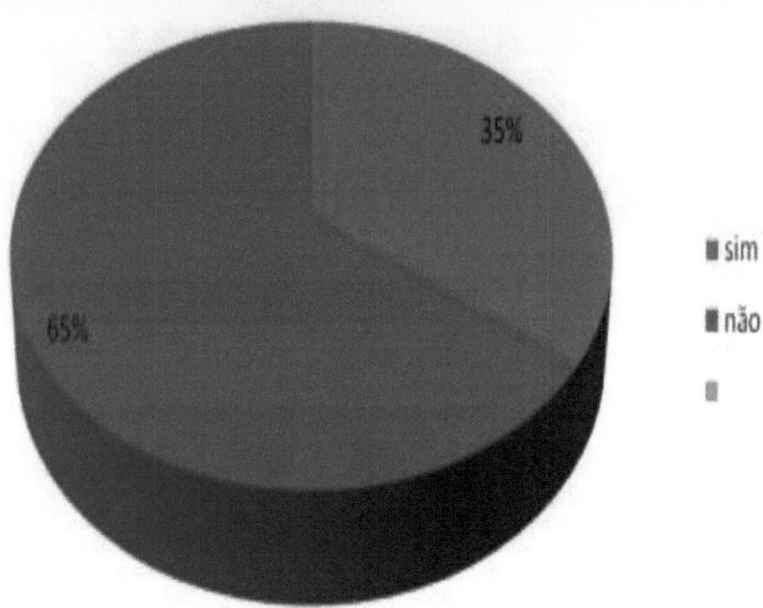

Do you complain about indiscipline in your classroom to your mother or father? The answers obtained were: 65% of the students said that they don't complain about classroom indiscipline to their parents and 35% said that they do complain about classroom indiscipline to their parents. Indiscipline in the classroom has become commonplace, a routine that often gets in the way, and yet students don't think it's necessary for their parents to intervene, a fact that is considered a concern for teachers

Graph 9: Result of whether student indiscipline influences the teacher's lesson preparation. Research by Tatiane Salvador da Cruz Tavares, 2012.

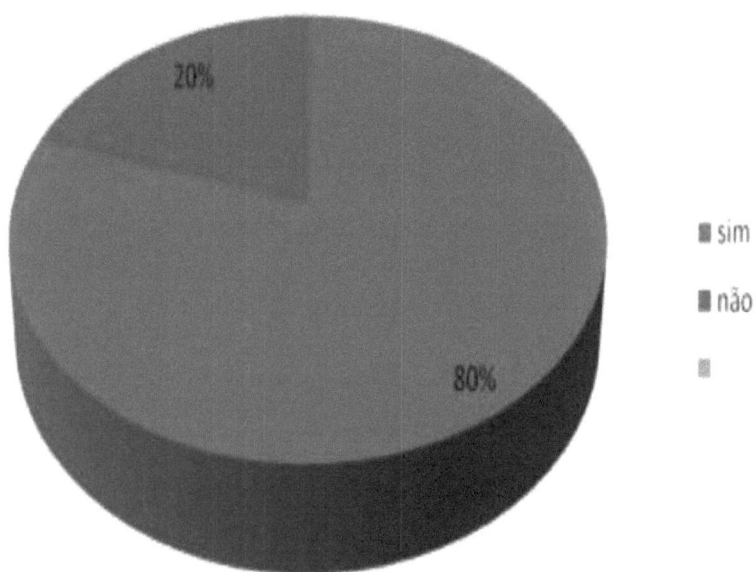

Among the answers obtained, 80% of the students believe that student behavior influences the teacher's lesson preparation and 20% believe that student behavior does not influence lesson preparation. The majority of students are aware that indiscipline hinders learning, which is why teachers need to adapt the content to the methodology used to improve student performance. It is necessary to draw up lesson plans specifically for a particular class, in order to involve them and thus obtain better learning results.

In research carried out in 2012 by researcher ALDAIR DE JESUS in his article: INDISCIPLINE IN THE CLASSROOM. A STUDY OF CAU SAS, MANAGEMENT DIFFICULTIES AND CONTROL STRATEGIES IN THE CLASS OF 5ª SERIES B OF PRIMARY EDUCATION. The following data was obtained:

Graph 10: Knowledge of school rules. Survey by Aldair de Jesus in 2012.

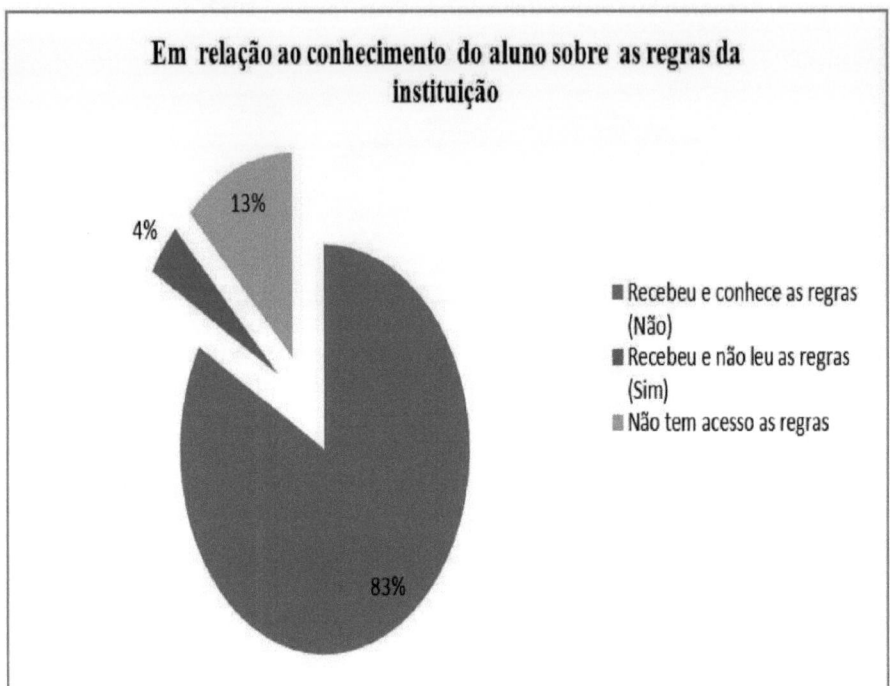

It can be seen that 83% of the students have not received and do not recognize the school rules, 13% say they do not have access to the rules and 4% have received the school rules but have never read them.

Graph 11: Who students blame for classroom indiscipline. Survey conducted by Aldair de Jesus in 2012.

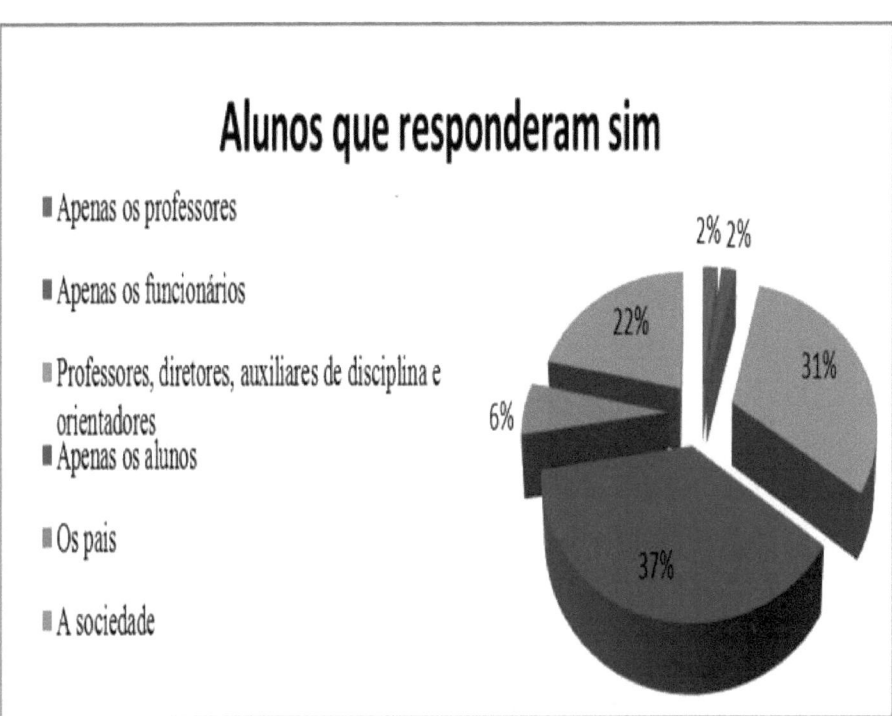

For 37% of the students, indiscipline is the fault of the students themselves, 31% blame the teachers, principals, discipline assistants and guidance counselors, 22% attribute indiscipline to society, 6% blame the parents, 2% blame the teachers and 2% blame the staff.

Alunos que responderam não

■ Apenas os professores

■ Apenas os funcionários

■ Professores, diretores, auxiliares de
   disciplina e orientadores
■ Apenas os alunos

■ Os pais

■ A sociedade

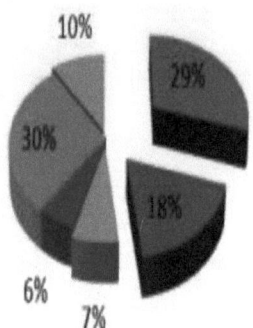

It can be seen that 29% of the students do not consider only teachers as contributing agents to their indiscipline; they also present a percentage of 18% for the staff as not stimulating this indiscipline; and they present 7% for the group that makes up the school educational organization: teachers, principals, discipline assistants and guidance counselors as not motivating the object studied. For themselves, 6% said that they were not responsible for their indiscipline; for their parents, 30% said that they did not blame them; and 10% said that society was not to blame for their students' indiscipline. In view of the above, if we analyze what was said in the the percentage given to themselves and to the group that makes   up the school organization, we can see that only a minority answered that they are not to blame for their indiscipline, with a percentage   of 6% and 7% respectively, This confirms the analysis discussed in the previous graph and leads us to   conclude that if, in the previous graph, 31% of the educational group and 37% of the students voted as guilty, the minority would certainly exempt them from blame, as we can see in the graph in question.

Graph 13: Results of who misbehaving students are raised by. Survey by Aldair de Jesus in 2012.

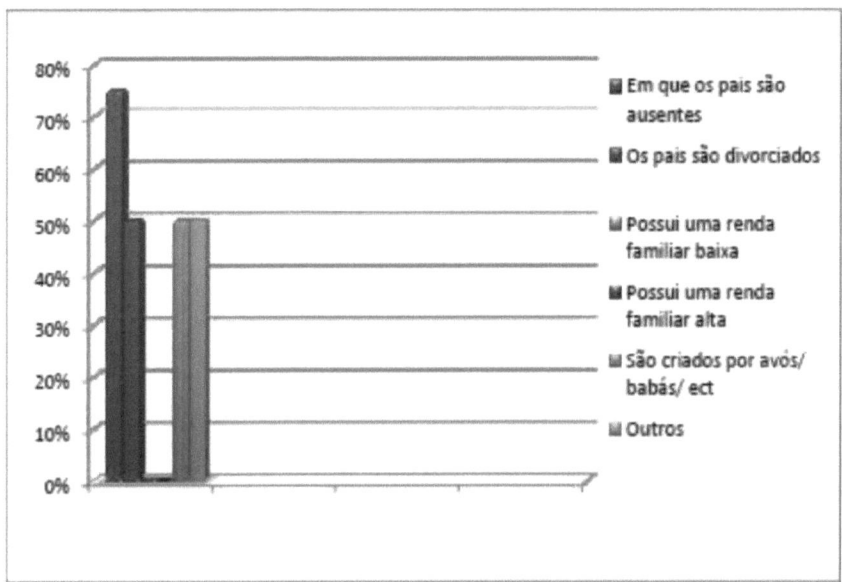

According to graph 13, 20% of the participants say that the child's behavior is unruly because the parents are absent, 13% when the parents are divorced and when the child is under the care of a third party. None of the participants say that the family's purchasing power influences the student's discipline.

Graph 14: Result if the child takes problems from home into the classroom. Survey by Aldair de Jesus in 2012

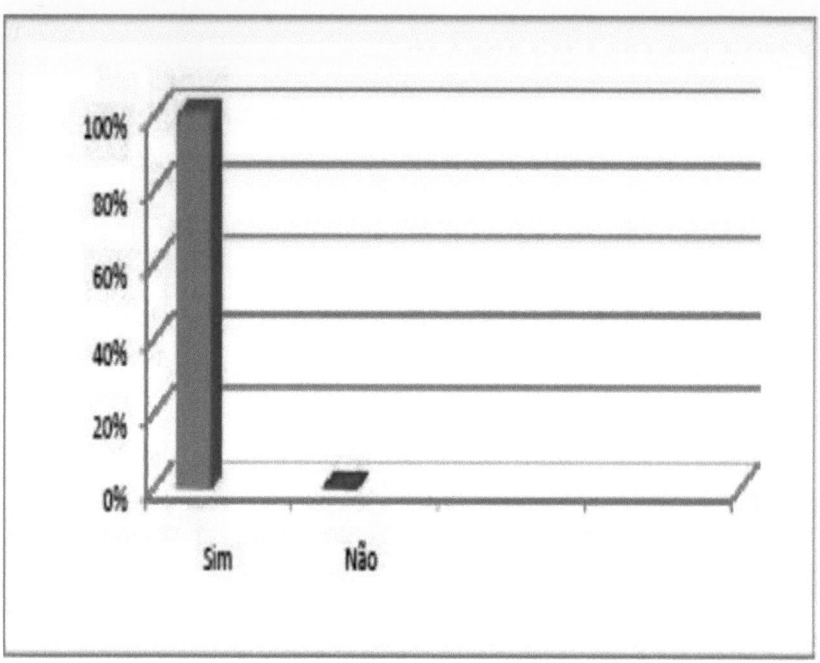

The graph shows that 100% of the children reflect the problems that happen at home in the classroom.

Many children show their feelings clearly: when they're sad, if they're nervous, if there's something they don't like, they show it in the way they act. Consequently, when a student is behaving unruly, especially when it is different from what they are used to, it may be that they are going through some emotional problem or even a family conflict that is causing changes in their attitudes.

Graph 15: Result of which child adapts best to school. Survey conducted by Aldair de Jesus in 2012.

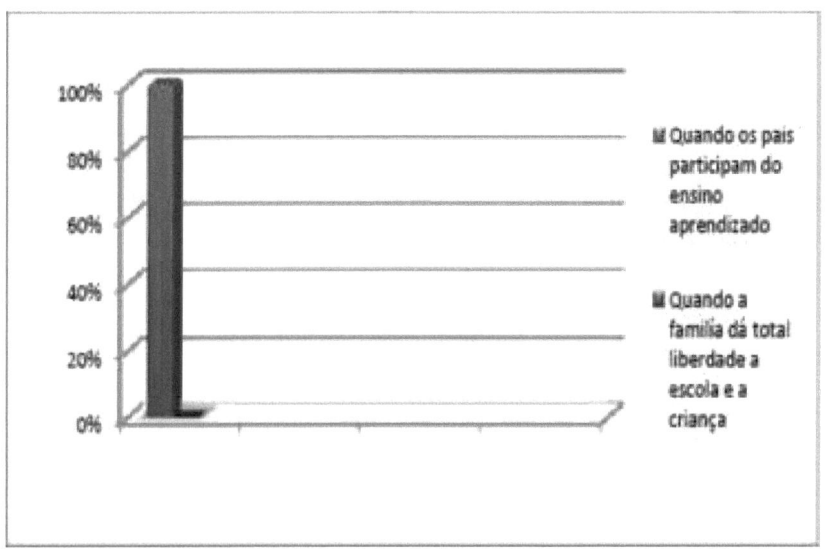

For 100% of the students surveyed, the children who adapt best to school are those whose parents are involved in their learning.

In a research study carried out by researcher Jakeliny Kelly Pinheiro da Fonseca, in her article: Indiscipline at School: Pedagogical Knowledge and Practice in the School Context, published in 2014, the following results were obtained:

Graph 16 - The presence of indiscipline at school. Jakeliny Kelly Pinheiro da Fonseca, 2014.

PRESENÇA DA INDISCIPLINA NA ESCOLA

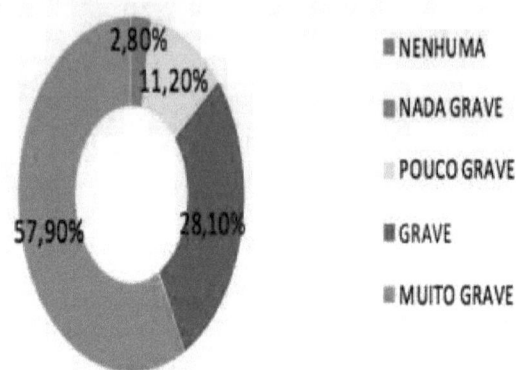

As can be seen, the presence of indiscipline in the school environment is a major issue. 57.90% of those interviewed answered that the presence of indiscipline in their school is very serious, while only 2.80% of those interviewed answered that indiscipline in their school is not serious.

The aim of this question was to encourage teachers and students to reflect critically on themselves, giving them the opportunity to evaluate their conduct in the classroom. This process was carried out with students from primary and secondary schools, and consisted of open and closed questions. The following results were obtained:

Graph 17 - Factors that influence indiscipline in the classroom. Research by Jakeliny Kelly Pinheiro da Fonseca, 2014.

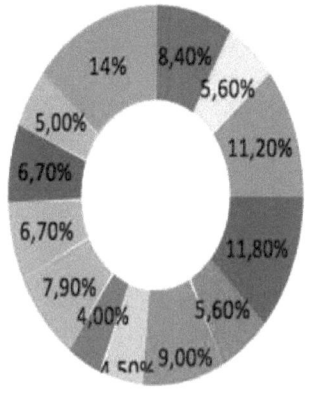

■ Alunos Inquietos

Alunos que não cooperam com o professor

■ Alunos quase sempre destraídos

■ Alunos que trocam msn. E bilhetinhos

■ Alunos com comp. Violento

■ Alunos que se ausentam com freq. Da sala

Alunos que interrompem as aulas com atitudes agressivas

■ Alunos que não gostam de trab. Em grupo

■ Alunos que se mostram desenteressados

Alunos que falam em voz alta

■ Alunos que gozam dos colegas e professores

Alunos que fazem perguntas impertinentes durante a aula

■ Alunos que não acatam as ordens dos professores

FATORES QUE INFLUENCIAM PARA A INDISCIPLINA NA SALA DE AULA

14%   8,40%
5,60%
5,00%
11,20%
6,70%
6,70%
11,80%
7,90%
4,00%   5,60%
4,50%   9,00%

According to the results obtained, it can be seen that these cases are the most commonly diagnosed in the classroom and that they promote inappropriate behavioral actions in everyday school life, resulting in many disagreements between students and teachers.

5.1 Comparative data on indiscipline in Brazilian schools compared to foreign schools

A survey carried out by the Organization for Economic Co-operation and Development (OECD) and published by the website G1.com, shows that in Brazil teachers spend 20% of their lesson time calming down students and getting the class in order in order to teach. In addition, the study shows that 60% of the Brazilian teachers interviewed have more than 10% problem students in their classroom, the highest rate among the countries participating in the study.

The Teaching and Learning International Survey (Talis) listened to teachers from 33 countries.

The study shows that in Brazil teachers spend 20% of their time putting the class in order and getting rid of the mess, 13% of their time solving bureaucratic problems and 67% teaching content. It's the country where teachers waste the most class time. The average for OECD countries is 13% of the time spent breaking up a mess.

The study asked teachers whether they had more or less than 10% of problem students in their class. Brazil had 60% of teachers saying they had more than 10% of problem students. Chile, Mexico and the United States follow. At the other end of the spectrum, Denmark, Croatia, Norway and Japan have fewer reports from teachers about students with bad behavior.

The data was collected in 2013 with primary and secondary school students (11 to 16 year olds), but a report on the issue of student behavior was released this year. In Brazil, 14,291 teachers and 1,057 principals from 1,070 schools completed the survey questionnaire.

The Talis survey collects data on the learning environment and working conditions of teachers in schools around the world. The aim is to provide information that can be compared with other countries in order to define policies for the development of education.

SOME DATA FROM THE SURVEY:

Time to put the class in order

In Brazil, teachers spend 20% of their time calming students down, scolding them and getting the class in order. The OECD average is 13%.

Students who arrive late.

This is not a big problem compared to other countries. The rate in Brazil is 51.4%, lower than the country average of 51.8%. More developed countries have students who fall behind more, such as Finland (86.5%), Sweden (78.4%), the Netherlands (75.7%), the United States (73.3%) and France (61.6%).

Missing school

Brazil is also on average, with 38.4%. Sweden (67.2%), Finland (64%) and Canada (61.8) have higher figures. The lowest index is in the Czech Republic (5.7%).

Vandalism and theft

Brazil is in second place in this item, with 11.8% of teachers' reports, behind Mexico, the leader with 13.2% and ahead of Malaysia, with 10.8%.

Verbal bullying between students

Brazil leads the survey with 34.4% of teacher reports, followed by Sweden (30.7%) and Belgium (30.7%).

Injuries in student brawl

Mexico has the highest rate (10.8%), followed by Cyprus (7.2%) and Finland (7%). Brazil comes fourth with 6.7%.

Verbal bullying of teachers

Brazil is in first place with 12.5%. Next comes Estonia (11%).

Use and possession of drugs and/or alcohol

In the reports, Brazil has the highest rate (6.9%), followed by Canada (6%).

Teacher training

Researcher Gabriela Moriconi, from the Carlos Chagas Foundation, took part in the survey. She also carried out research in Ontario, Canada, and England, and found that teacher training is better in these countries.

Also according to the study, in Brazil, more than 90% of teachers in the final years of elementary school have completed higher education, but around 25% have not taken a teacher training course. By comparison, in Chile approximately 9 out of 10 teachers have completed such courses, as have almost all teachers in Australia and Alberta (Canada).

"In Brazil, because of problems with salaries and other activities, a teacher is put in place who hasn't been prepared to teach that subject. What's more, the average in Brazil is 31 students per class, while in other countries it's 24," says Gabriela.

According to her, it is necessary to create a system for planning support policies for schools and teachers to deal with students who are developing. "Everyone understands that in pre-adolescence students test their limits and are learning to be autonomous," says the researcher. "Before we think that our students are doing well, we need to see that in other countries students have a lot of support that they don't have in our country."

In her report, the researcher concludes that "building a positive school culture can be a way to reduce behavior problems and absenteeism, and therefore improve students' learning conditions". "One way to create a more positive environment is to involve students, parents and teachers in school decisions. Teachers who work in schools with a higher level of stakeholder participation have fewer reports of students with behavioral problems in their classrooms."

5.2 Ideas and suggestions on how to combat indiscipline

The following text provides some suggestions from the authors AQUINO, Julio Groppa

(1996) and LEMOV, Doug (2011) for dealing with indiscipline in the classroom.

> **Set the rules from the first day of school**: "The first impression is the one that sticks". Who doesn't know this saying? Well, it translates exactly the attitude that teachers should have from the first day of class.

> **Dictate the rules of the game so that students know how to play**: Saying what is expected of the child or adolescent is the first step in getting them to do what is set out.

> **Make sure your students know what they can and can't do**:

The rules must be clear and everyone must know them. After all, it's easy to make a mistake when you don't know any of the rules, and that's how controversies are created, as it opens up space for "he-said-she-said".

> **Take on the school rules**: If the school sets rules and the teacher doesn't follow them, why would a student follow a rule set by the teacher?

> **Don't discourage your students**: Be professional. Take on the rules of your educational institution, together with all the staff.

> **Don't be late**: A teacher who is often late when he or she arrives is a disappointment to the student.

> **A good teacher is not an educator**: Educating is pruning. Anyone who is a parent knows very well how many "naos" are said daily to their most precious treasure.

> **Assume that the difficult student is a pedagogical challenge and not "a pain in the ass"**: Who hasn't witnessed teachers venting at break time? Usually difficult pupils, those who annoy us and get on our nerves, become a pain in the ass and we end up blaming them.

> **Distinguish the rules**: indiscipline is the transgression of two types of rule: those of a moral nature (based on ethical principles, aimed at the common good, and therefore valid for all institutions and for any situation, such as not hitting, not swearing and not lying) and those of a conventional nature (which vary from school to school, such as those relating to the use of cell phones, uniforms and caps). Often   , school regulations make a mistake in placing these

two situations on the same level. It is important to distinguish between them in order to better understand   and deal with discipline.

> **Conquering authority**: Every time you try to impose discipline with authoritarianism,

50

revolt ensues. With more knowledge, every teacher gains confidence in the teaching content and learns to plan effective lessons. It may sound simple, but it is essential for maintaining discipline and ensuring that everyone learns.

> **Encouraging cooperation**: Striving to build a quality school climate in which students are respected and learn to respect brings rewards: appropriate behavior because everyone is aware of their role at school and not because they are afraid of punishment. In this situation, teachers and managers are seen as figures of moral and intellectual authority, capable of fair negotiations with the kids (never authoritarian).

> **Act calmly:** In a situation of indiscipline, it is necessary to express dissatisfaction. Without getting carried away, showing the student that the whole group is affected will help them realize the consequences of their actions and learn how to act in other similar situations.

> **Always be alert:** It is up to the school to cultivate an atmosphere of cooperation and respect, as it is to be expected that cases of indiscipline will always arise. Even if the staff is trained to act more confidently in dealing with the problem, there will always be new teachers and students, who will need time to adjust to this way of dealing with conflicts.

> **Stimulating autonomy: Sometimes** students act unruly to show that a rule isn't working. In some cases, they want to draw attention to their own ideas. By living in an environment based on respect and negotiating rules, students learn to make responsible decisions.

> **Recognize the qualities of difficult students**: Express positivity to each of your students on a daily basis. No matter how difficult they are, always interact with them in a welcoming way.

> **Use encouraging phrases during the lesson**: Phrases that motivate students help them connect with the lesson and the content. After all, many difficult students are just looking for a little approval. Look for opportunities to use this type of phrase during the day.

> **See the "worst student" as the best:** Think of your best student. Who is the best behaved? The most motivated? What adjectives come to mind when talking about this child?

Observe how you interact with this student and try acting in the same way with the other misbehaving student for a week. See what happens with this change in treatment.

> **Send progress reports to parents: Write** a letter or email that briefly describes to parents the progress the student is making

in relation to their behavior. Show them that you are seeing progress and have good expectations for their child.

> **Use games**: Games increase the child's interest in education due to the novelty factor, emphasize the importance of following the rules, sociability and self-knowledge - after all, to win you need to know the rules, your opponent and yourself.

Twenty steps to combat indiscipline with students in the classroom:

1   - Establish clear rules

2   - Make your students understand them

3   - Determine a sanction for breaking them

4   - Determine a reward for compliance

5   - Ask your teammates for support

6   - Establish strategies together with the team; students need to realize the hegemony of attitudes

7   - Respect your students

8   - Listen to them

9   - Answer questions politely and patiently

10   - Praise good behavior

11   - Be clear and objective in your speeches

12   - Make it clear that it's the behavior that's wrong, not the student

13   - Be consistent in your expectations

14   - Recognize your students' feelings and respect them

15   - Don't tell them what to do; let them come to their own conclusions

16   - Don't unload your machine gun of sorrows on them

17   - Always encourage

18   - Believe in everyone's potential and in your own

19   - Work on negative beliefs by turning them into positive ones

20   - Be affectionate

6. CONCLUSION

In the course of this bibliographical study, it became clear that indiscipline is a problem that suffers from numerous influences, both external and internal to the school.

As a professional, teachers must always be up to date with new practices to minimize and/or solve this serious problem in everyday school life. They must be willing to abandon old, outdated disciplinary practices and manage current teaching models, taking into account the new student profile we have today. It is essential to recognize that students bring with them knowledge and experiences, that they have an active voice, that they demand and question, that they have doubts, and that these characteristics cannot be considered a problem, but are attributes required in various spheres of social experience.

One practice that teachers can try to tackle this problem is to use motivation as a way of ensuring that students pay attention and perform well at school. Through motivation, students will feel more stimulated and engaged in their schoolwork, thus making teaching and learning more enjoyable experiences for students and teachers alike, making them feel a sense of belonging and responsibility for the smooth running of activities in the school environment.

However, in tackling school indiscipline, education cannot be considered the responsibility of schools alone. Every social relationship can be and is learning in a positive or negative sense. Family relationships, the workplace, the media, politics, religions, in any sector of human activity, we are learning and teaching. The new generations use these models and proposals with technical, political and moral content. In this context,   the   school community needs to be made aware of the constant need for dialogue, not just with specialists, students and teachers, but with all those involved who are interested in the advancement of education and social relations.

It's clear that the major social and family changes brought about by the process of democratizing access to education have brought to our schools a public with different expectations and a very diverse behavioral reality. The school still struggles to treat as equals what is by nature unequal and individual. Families, on the other hand, are finding it difficult to monitor their children's development at school and are distancing themselves from the school.

Finally, it should be emphasized that everyone who takes part in the responsibility of educating must commit to working collectively so that the objectives can move in a single direction. Family, school, society, public policies, we are all responsible for forming new citizens who are aware of their role in society, in school and more than that: in history.

7. REFERENCES

ALMEIRA, Laurinda Ramalho de. (org). **Affectivity and learning**: Contributions from Henri Wallon. Sao Paulo: Ed. Loyola. 2007.

ALMEIDA, Daniele. **On the brink of chaos**. Nova Escola, n. 218, p. 84-87, Dec. 2008.

AMADO, Joao da Silva. **Pedagogical interaction and indiscipline in the classroom**. Porto: Asa, 2001.

Amado, J. S., & Freire, I. P. (2009). **School indiscipline(s): Understanding to prevent**. Coimbra: Almedina

AQUINO, Julio Gropa. **The teacher-student relationship: from the pedagogical to the institutional**. Sao Paulo: Summus, 1996.

AQUINO, J. G. **Confrontos na sala de aula: uma leitura institucional da relaçâo professor-aluno**. 2ª ed. Sao Paulo: Summus, 1996.

AQUINO, J. G. **Indiscipline at school: theoretical and practical alternatives**. Sao Paulo: Summus, 1996.

AQUINO, Julio Groppa. **Indiscipline and today's school**. Rev. Fac. Educ, Sao Paulo, v. 24, n.2,   1998.

AQUINO, Julio Gropa. **The teacher-student relationship: from the pedagogical to the institutional**. Sao Paulo: Summus, 1996.

AQUINO, J. G. **Confrontos na sala de aula: uma leitura institucional da relaçâo professor-aluno**. 2a ed. Sao Paulo: Summus, 1996.

AQUINO, J. G. **Indiscipline at school: theoretical and practical alternatives**. Sao Paulo: Summus, 1996.

AQUINO, Julio Groppa. **Indiscipline and today's school**. Rev. Fac. Educ. Sao Paulo, v. 24, n.2, 1998.

AQUINO, Julio G. (eds.) **Indiscipline at School: theoretical and practical alternatives** . In: LAJONQUIÉRE, Leandro de. **Children, "their" (in)discipline and psychoanalysis**.

In: TAILLE, Yves de La. **Indiscipline and the feeling of shame**. Sao Paulo: Sumus, 1996, 148 p.

ARROYO, M. G. **Oficio de mestre: imagens e auto-imagens**. Petrópolis: Vozes, 2000.

BLAYA, C. (Org). Violence in schools and public policies. Brasilia: UNESCO. 2002.

BOARINI, Maria Lucia. **School discipline: a collective construction**. Revista Semestral Da Associaçao Brasileira de Psicologia Escolar e Educacional. Maringà, v.17, n.1, Jan. - Jun. 2013. p.123-131. Disponivel em: http://dx.doi.org/10.1590/S1413-85572013000100013. Accessed on: September 15, 2016.

CARRAHER, Terezinha Nunes. **Society and intelligence**. Sao Paulo: Cortez, 1989; CARRAHER, David William; SCHLIEMANN, Analûcia. *In life ten, in school zero*. Sao Paulo: Cortez, 1993.

CHUi, Marilena. **Convite á filosofia**. 12. ed. Sao Paulo: Ed. Atica, 2000.

CHUi, Marilena. **Convite á filosofia**. 12. ed. Sao Paulo: Ed. Atica, 2000.

COLL, César; Alvaro Narchesi, Jesús Palacios et al. **Psychological development and education: developmental disorders and special educational needs**. 2^a Ed. Vol. 3. Artmed. 2004.

DAMETTO, J. ; ESQUINSANI, R. S. S. **The School as a locus for the emergence of subjective disparities**: **Power, Knowledge and Resistance in Formal Education**. In: SILVA, Jacqueline Silva da; LOPES, Maria Isabel. (Org.). **Disciplina: relações de poder na Escola**. Lageado-RS: Univates, 2009. p. 13-28.

DEBARBIEUX E, **Violence in schools: disagreements over words and a political challenge**. Page 59. In: DEBARBIEUX, E. and BLAYA, C. (Org) Violence in schools and public policies. Brasilia: UNESCO. 2002.

http://unesdoc.unesco.org/images/0012/001287/128720por.pdf, accessed on October 20, 2016.

DE LA TAILLE, Yves. **Indiscipline and the feeling of shame**. In: AQUINO, J. G. (Org.) **Indisciplina na escola: alternativas teóricas e praticas**. 8. ed. Sao Paulo: Summus, 1996.

(DICIONARIO DE PSICOLOGIA, p. 439).

ECCHELI, Simone D. **Motivation as the prevention of indiscipline**. Educar em revista. Curitiba, n. 32, p.199-213. 2008 . Available at:

http://www.scielo.br/scielo.php?script=sci_arttext&pid=S0104-40602008000200014&lang=pt. Accessed on: September 10, 2016

ESTRELA, Maria. Tereza. **Pedagogical** relationship**, discipline and indiscipline in the classroom**. 3. ed. Porto: Porto, 1992.

ESTRELA, Maria Teresa. **Pedagogical relationship, discipline and indiscipline in the classroom**. 4. ed. Porto: Porto, 2002.

FERNANDEZ, I. Prevención de la violencia y resolución de conflictos: el clima esco- lar como factor de calidad. Madrid: Nancea. 2004.

FURLANI, L.M.T. **Teacher authority: Goal, myth or nothing** at all? Sao Paulo. Editora Cortez. 2004.

FREIRE, Paulo. **Pedagogy of autonomy: knowledge necessary for educational learning**. Sao Paulo: Paz e Terra. 1997.

FREIRE, P. **Pedagogy of the Oppressed**. 17th ed. Rio de Janeiro, Paz e Terra, 1987.

FREIRE, P. **Educaçâo como pràtica da liberdade**. 19 ed. Rio de Janeiro: Paz e Terra, 1989.

FREIRE, Paulo. **Pedagogy of autonomy: knowledge necessary for educational practice"**. Sao Paulo: Editora Paz e Terra, 1996.

FREITAG, B. **Escola, Estado e sociedade**. 4. ed. Sao Paulo: Moraes, 1980.

FRELLER, Cintia Copit. **Stories of school indiscipline: the work of a psychologist from a Winnicottian perspective**. 2. ed. Sao Paulo: Casa do Psi- cólogo, 2008.

FONSECA, Jakeliny Kelly Pinheiro. **Pedagogical Knowledge and Practice in the School Context**. Sao Paulo, 2014.

FURLANI, L.M.T. **Teacher authority: Goal, myth or nothing** at all? Sao Paulo. Editora Cortez. 2004.

GARCIA, Joe. **Indiscipline at school**. Revista Paranaense de Desenvolvimento, Curitiba, n. 95, p. 101-108, jan./abr. 1999.

GOLDANI, Andrea. TOGATLIAN, Marco Aùrelio. COSTA, Rosane de Albuquerque. **Development, Emotion and Relationships at School**. Rio de Janeiro: Epapers, 2010.

GOTIZENS, C. **School discipline: prevention and intervention in behavior problems** 2. ed. Porto Alegre: Artmed, 2003.

GUIMARAES, Aurea M. **Vigilância, puniçâo e depredaçâo escolar**. Campinas, Sao Paulo, Papirus, 1985.

HAYDT, Regina Célia. **Course in general didactics**. 2nd ed. Sao Paulo: Atica, 1995.

JESUS, Saul Neves de. **How can teacher stress and student indiscipline be** prevented and resolved? *Cadernos do CRIAP,* Portugal: Ediçôes Asa, p. 44-62, 1999.

JESUS, Saul Neves de. **Strategies to motivate students**. Educaçâo. Porto Alegre, n. 31, p. 21-29, Jan./Apr. 2008.

JESUS, Aldair de. **Indiscipline in the classroom, a study of the causes, management difficulties and control strategies in the class of 5ª grade b of elementary school**, Sâo Paulo, 2012.

JUSTO, José Sterza. **School at the epicenter of the social crisis**. In: LA TAYLLE, Yves de. (Org.) **Indisciplina/disciplina: ética, moral e açâo do professor**. Porto Alegre: Mediaçâo, 2010.p.23-54.

LAJONQUIÉRE, Leandro de. **The child, "his" (in)discipline and psychoanalysis**. In: TAILLE, Yves de La. **Indiscipline and the feeling of shame**. Sâo Paulo: Su- mus, 1996.

LEMOV, Doug. **Aula Nota 10: 49 techniques to be a top teacher**. 4ª ed. Sâo Paulo: Da Boa Prosa, 2011.

LIBÂNEO, José Carlos. Didactics. Sâo Paulo: Cortez Editora, 1994.

MAIA, Heber. **Neuroeducation and pedagogical actions**. Ana Teresa Perdomo Molter (et al); Heber Maia (org). Rio de Janeiro: Walk Editora, 2011.

MAIA, Heber, **Special Educational Needs**. Adriana Rocha Brito (et al); Heber Maia (org). Rio de Janeiro: Walk Editora, 2011.

MALDONADO, Maria Tereza. **Communication between parents and children:** the language of feeling. 8. ed. Petrópolis: Vozes, 2001.

MELLO, Tàgides; RUBIO, Juliana de Alcântara Silveira. **The Importance of Affectivity in the Teacher/Student Relationship in the Teaching/Learning Process in Early Childhood Education**. Saberes da Educaçâo Electronic Journal. Vol.4 N°1 2013 ISNN 2177-7748   Available: http://www.facsaoroque.br/novo/publicacoes/pdf/v4-n1-2013/Tagides.pdf Accessed on: 10/02/2017.

MENDES, F. **A indisciplina em aulas de educaçao fisica no 6° ano de escolaridade - Contribuindo para o estudo dos comportamentos de indisciplina do aluno e análise dos procedimentos de controle utilizados pelo professor**. PhD thesis, Faculty of Sports Sciences and Physical Education. University of Porto, 1995.

OECD (2015), **Education at a Glance 2015:** OECD Indicators, OECD Publishing, Paris, http://dx.doi.org/10.1787/eag- 2015-en.

OLIVEIRA, Rosimary Lima Guilherme. **Teachers' attitudes towards school indiscipline.** 2004.   189. Dissertation (Master's Degree in Education). Faculties of Human Sciences, Letters and Arts - Tuiuti University of Paranà, Curitiba, 2004.

RODRIGUES, Joana Maria Di santo. Brasil Escola magazine, 2014. Available at: http://monografias.brasilescola.uol.com.br/educacao/provaveis-causas-que-familia-influencia-na-indisciplina-escolar.htm access: Feb.2017.

SANTO, Joana Maria Rodrigues Di. **Discipline at School: Challenging Task and Construction.**   Available   at: http://www.centrorefeducacional.com.br/monojoana2.htm. Accessed on: 07 Feb. 2017.

Schaffer, H. Rudolph (2005). **Introduction to child psychology.** Lisbon: Piaget Institute.

SIQUEIRA, Alessandra Maria de Oliveira; NETO, Demuniz Diniz da Silva; FLORÊN- CIA, Rutemara. A **Importância da Afetividade da Aprendizagem dos Alunos**, Fa- culdade de Ciências, Educaçâo e Teologia do Norte do Brasil. 2011. Available at: http://www.faceten.edu.br/Importancia%20da%20afetividade%20na%20aprendizage m.pdf Accessed on: 11/02/2017 STEMME, Fritz. The Power of Emotions. Sâo Paulo: Cultrix LTDA. n.d.

TAVARES, Tatiane Salvador da Cruz. **Indiscipline at school and its influence on learning**, Sâo Paulo, 2012.

TIBA, Içami. Discipline: **limits in the right measure. New paradigms /** Içami Tiba. - Ver. Atual e ampli. - Sâo Paulo: Integrare Editora, 2006.

TIBA, Içami. Adolescents: Who Loves, Educates! Sao Paulo: Ed. Integrare, 2005

. Discipline, Limit in the Right Measure. Sao Paulo: Gente, 1996, 1st ed.

. Who Loves, Educates! Sao Paulo: Gente, 2002

VASCONCELOS C. dos Santos. **Where is the teacher going? Rescuing the teacher as a subject of transformation.**10. Ed. Sâo Paulo: Libertad , 2003.

VASCONCELLOS, Celso dos Santos. (In) Disciplina: **Construçâo da disciplina consciente e interactiva em sala de aula e na escola.** Sâo Paulo: Libertad Editora, 2004.

VASCONCELLOS, Celso dos Santos. **Discipline:** building conscious and interactive discipline in the classroom and at school. 7. ed. Sao Paulo: Libertad, 1995.

60

Veiga, F. (2001). **Indiscipline and violence at school. Communication practices for teachers and parents**. Coimbra: Almedina.

http://g1.globo.com/educacao/noticia/2015/03/professor-no-brasil-perde-20-da-aula- com-bagunca-na-classe-diz-estudo.html . access on 04/06/2017

Printed by Books on Demand GmbH, Norderstedt / Germany